MUCHA

T&J

This edition published 2011

Published by
TAJ BOOKS INTERNATIONAL LLP
27 Ferndown Gardens
Cobham
Surrey
KT11 2BH
UK
www.tajbooks.com

All notations of errors or omissions (author inquiries, permissions) concerning the content of this book should be addressed to info@tajbooks.com.

ISBN: 978-1-84406-171-6

MUCHA

BY SANDRA FORTY

ALPHONSE MUCHA 1860–1939

The artist who came to symbolize all the excitement, exoticism, glamor, and allure of Paris of the late nineteenth century was born halfway across Eastern Europe in the small, rather isolated town of Ivančice in Southern Moravia, in what is now the Czech Republic but was then in the Austrian Empire. At the height of his fame at the turn of the twentieth century he was the talk of the Parisian salons with much of the gossip speculating on his ethnic origin—was he Spanish or Hungarian?—even though Mucha himself made it explicit that he was Moravian. In fact, one popular story had him being stolen from a gypsy camp by Sarah Bernhardt herself!

Mucha specialized in lithographs of strongly linear composition, most of which were of women with sensuous curves, all enclosed within elegant, refined, decorative floral elements. His women had long elaborately folded robes, luscious, sinuous hair, exotic jewels, and more often than not, a halo around their head celebrating their otherworldly magnificence. They were surrounded with elegantly entwined flowers and numerous symbols taken from almost every lexicon of pattern from around the world. Much of this was couched in a gold-enhanced Byzantine style with strange occult overtones. All his works were executed with supreme confidence and utter mastery of line. The effect at the time was totally original and took the French public, in particular, by storm. His work also stood out from other artists by his use of muted subtle color and soft tones.

Alphonse (Alfons) Maria Mucha was born in 1860 in central Europe to a local court official and his second wife, a retired governess. Local legend had it that he could draw—hold a crayon, anyway—before he could walk. His mother hoped he would become a priest but as a young schoolboy his musical talent meant he could progress to high school in Brünn (present day Brno), the capital of Moravia. There he learned to play music and became a choirboy for three years, which gave him long hours to study and appreciate all the ecclesiastical art surrounding him.

When his voice broke Mucha had to leave the choir and so was sent by his father to follow in his own footsteps and become a (not very good) clerk in the local courthouse. In his spare time he designed sets for the local amateur theater as well as doing a little acting and producing. This—much to his parents' dismay—opened his eyes to the possibility of making art his future with the inevitable dream of moving to Paris, the heart of the contemporary art world. With the support of his drawing teacher Mucha applied to become a student at the Academy of Fine Arts in Prague, but he was not accepted. He still dreamed of Paris but the city was 650 miles away and an all but impossible ambition.

Instead, at the age of 17 in 1879, Mucha moved to Vienna, the capital of the Austrian Empire, to work as a scene painter for Kautsky-Brioschi-Burghardt, suppliers of theatrical scenery, backcloths, and curtains, especially to the famous Ringtheater. He remained there until a terrible fire in December 1881 destroyed the theater and killed some 500 people; without the Ringtheater the firm was forced to drastically reduce its staff, including Mucha.

Mucha, seen seated, just before the opening of his Slav Epic exhibition at the Klememtimum in Prague, 1919.

Although unemployed, Mucha remained in Vienna as long as possible until his money ran out, then he bought a rail ticket, at random, to the town of Mikulov where he moved into a hotel and started to sell the odd drawing to the local bookseller. Soon he had regular work drawing portraits of the townswomen and in his spare time he also got involved with Mikulov's theater where he painted scenery, played the violin and guitar, and did the odd bit of acting. His social life blossomed and he met many people including the manager of the local grand estate that was owned by the hugely wealthy Count Karl Khuen. After seeing some of his work the count invited Mucha to come and live at newly built Emmahof Castle near Hrusovany and paint a series of decorative frescoes for the dining room.

Although he had never before painted in fresco Mucha quickly learned the technique and started the commission, while at the same time enjoying the luxuries of the castle, especially its library full of art and history books. When the job was completed the count gave him another commission at his family castle at Gandegg in the Tyrol, where his brother and amateur painter Count Egon lived. Together they redecorated much of the castle. After two years working for Count Khuen, Mucha was advised to apply to the Academy of Fine Arts in Munich: he sat the entrance exam in 1885 and was accepted as a third-year student with the count acting as his patron and sponsor.

Mucha enjoyed life as a student and even though the teaching was very traditional, the sessions encouraged his love of historic painting. At the end of the course, Mucha returned to Emmahof Castle to fresco the billiard room. Delighted with the results, Count Khuen agreed to continue funding Mucha's studies and enquired whether he would prefer Paris or Rome. Mucha chose the former, although he did not speak a word of French, with the arrangement that Count Khuen would send him 200 francs a month and in return Mucha would send him drawings and regular progress reports.

At last in 1887 Mucha arrived in Paris where he enrolled at the Académie Julian. He started learning French and although he worked hard at his studies, he spent much of his free time with other Czech ex-patriots longing for home. For the summer vacation Mucha returned to Emmahof and more fresco work, then on his return to Paris he enrolled at the Académie Colarossi and took lodgings on the Rive Gauche.

Count Karl paid Mucha's way for two years but in 1889 withdrew the funding for reasons unknown, leaving Mucha at the age of 27 without a sou. With no money coming in, Mucha had to leave the Académie and find work as an illustrator. Throughout his student years he had composed advertising posters and contributed illustrations to magazines and he continued such work as he could get for the next five years. His first life-saving commission was a series of illustrations for *Le Petit Parisien Illustré*.

Mucha was now living the classic starving artist's life, living from hand to mouth in a squalid room and existing much of the time on a diet of lentils. This bohemian but impoverished life improved when a Polish student friend named Slewinsky found him new lodgings in a room above Madame Charlotte's Crémerie, a restaurant for students, in the rue de la Grande Chaumière. There he mingled with other like-minded young artists and picked up occasional illustrating work, in particular the weekly cover for *La Vie Populaire* magazine and illustrations for a book of fairy stories for Xavier Marmier which garnered him an Honorable Mention from the Salon. Still he barely managed to feed himself and once almost died of an illness caused by his poverty.

Late nineteenth century Paris was a thriving, exciting time for artists: the Impressionists had become fashionable and the artistic movements of the Decadents and Symbolists were just starting. Mucha seemingly knew everyone in that rarefied circle and in 1891 became friends with Gauguin. But Gauguin was soon off to the South Seas after a sale of his paintings scraped together enough money for the journey. They renewed their friendship on his return two years later and Gauguin took a corner of Mucha's studio; Madame Charlotte was sharp enough to buy some of Gauguin's paintings. All the while Mucha was developing and refining his artistic style and also started giving art lessons to the students who frequented the Crémerie.

During this period Mucha illustrated for various publications including the *Revue Mame, L'Illustration, Figaro Illusive* and the bible of the Parisian entertainment scene, *Le Costume au Théâtre*. The latter gave him access to free theatre, entertainment tickets across Paris, and an introduction to many of the influential producers and publishers of the city; in turn resulting in many offers of further work. Perhaps the most prestigious of these was the opportunity presented by

ALPHONSE MUCHA 1860–1939

the publisher Armand Colin to contribute drawings for his 41-part serialization of the history of Germany by Charles Seignobos, *Scenes et Episodes de l'histoire d'Allemagne*. Mucha designed 33 drawings that were turned into woodcuts after his studies by G. Lemoine. In 1894 four of the original drawings were exhibited at the Salon des Artistes Français and four years later, 27 were shown at the Galerie de la Bodinière.

Mucha's big break came at the end of 1894 when he chanced to visit the offices of the printer Lemercier, a print shop where one of his friends was employed. According to his own—no doubt highly romanticized and selectively remembered—account, Mucha was working there checking some lithography proofs over December 25 and 26 when, just as he finished, the print manager Monsieur de Brunoff rushed into the shop. He had just taken a call from the celebrated actress Sarah Bernhardt ordering a poster for her play that she needed by New Year's Day. The production, *Gismonda*, was flagging badly and she needed to give it a boost. All Lemercier's regular poster artists were away on vacation and so the job was offered to Mucha.

Bernhardt was the most celebrated actress in France and the opportunity to publicize her work was a rare opportunity for Mucha. First of all he had to meet her at the Théâtre de la Renaissance. For the occasion he hired a tailcoat, borrowed a friend's top hat, and rushed along taking his pencil and paper for sketching. Mucha was entranced by Madame Bernhardt and vowed to delight her with his work.

Back at Lemercier's, the manager De Brunoff had to go for his vacation leaving

Mucha unsupervised as he worked on two large lithographic stones for the next few days. The resulting poster was proofed up on December 30 and announced Sarah Bernhardt's appearance in *Gismonda* at the Théâtre de la Renaissance on the Boulevard Saint-Martin. De Brunoff on his return was deeply unconvinced by the result—a stunning, long, narrow, near life-size poster in unusually muted colors—and feared Bernhardt would reject the work and jeopardize his own job in the process. Nevertheless, there was no time for change and the poster was sent off for her inspection.

Thoroughly unnerved, Mucha sunk into depression as he waited in trepidation to hear the result. A phone call summoned him to attend Madame Bernhardt at the Boulevard Saint-Martin where—much to his relief—she told him she loved the Byzantine poster. The posters were put up all over Paris on January 1, 1895, and immediately attracted attention with the highly decorative and stylized design. It immediately became the sensation of Paris: excited crowds gathered around the posters to marvel at the innovative design. They tried to buy the posters from the poster men or attempted to remove them from the hoardings.

The work was in the developing Art Nouveau style, although Mucha himself always denied any influence from that quarter. The poster for *Gismonda* turned Mucha into an overnight sensation and suddenly everyone wanted his work and all of Paris wanted to know about him. Bernhardt herself was so thrilled that she contracted him for six years to not only design her posters, programs, and theater cards but all her sets and costumes as well. She ordered 4,000 more copies of *Gismonda* and sold them on herself for a profit. However, following a court case with Lemercier's over disputed deliveries, Bernhardt had the lithographic stones destroyed to preserve their exclusivity and moved all her business to rival printers Champenois in 1896 taking Mucha with her.

That year Mucha drew another poster of Bernhardt showing just her head and shoulders, wearing lilies in her hair. Again there is a halo around her head with her name emblazoned around the aurora that in turn is highlighted against a background of golden stars. This particular work was repeatedly used for her personal appearances rather than for specific named plays, and changed according to the occasion.

Suddenly commissions flooded in—for advertisements, book illustrations and jackets, magazine covers, paintings, interior decorations, jewelry, wallpaper, and of course, posters. He rapidly became the best-known artist of the Art Nouveau, a style also called the Mucha Style. Mucha's original approach was much copied but never bettered.

When he became more prosperous, Mucha moved to a bigger studio across the road at 6 rue du Val de Grace—and Gauguin moved to join him. Here he had room to work simultaneously on a number of large lithographic stones and indulge his new interest in photography. Mucha started photographing both his many friends and occasional professional models in a variety of poses. He made a famous study of Gauguin sitting without trousers at the studio beside his new harmonium.

With the increased volume of work,

especially his new commission to illustrate *Ilsee, Princesse de Tripoli* by Robert de Flers, Mucha employed skilled craftsmen to follow his original designs for his distinctive repetitive decorative motifs. This way, within three months, he was able to present the publisher, Piazza, with 134 colored lithographs, plus the cover art and the design of the book itself.

Over the next few years Mucha designed for Sarah Bernhardt some of the greatest lithographic posters ever produced: two in 1896, the first for the play *La Dame aux Camélias* and the second for *Lorenzaccio*, a tragedy by Alfred de Musset showing Bernhardt sombrely dressed in black robes. In 1897 he produced a poster for the verse play *La Samaritaine* and the following year a dramatic poster for the melodrama *Médée*. In 1899 Bernhardt played Hamlet in the adaptation *La Tragique Histoire de Hamlet, Prince de Danemark* and Mucha made the last of his great posters for her, showing her dressed as Hamlet in medieval tunic and cloak.

Mucha had become so celebrated that he had two major exhibitions in 1897: in February at the Galerie de la Bodinière and then in May at the Salon des Cent, one of the homes of the Symbolist art movement and the offshoot of the magazine *La Plume*. Mucha showed 448 works at the latter that was publicized by a poster he had made for the Salon two years earlier of a half-naked girl with flowing hair. Additionally *La Plume* published five consecutive special issues (later rebound into one volume) celebrating Mucha and cataloging his writings and artworks as well as other peoples' assessments of him.

By 1900 Mucha was one of the most-celebrated artists working in Paris and although Bernhardt kept him busy designing sets and costumes as well as posters, he found time to write two books about pattern making: *Documents Décoratives* and *Figures Décoratives*, widely read and hugely influential in the execution and depiction of contemporary popular art.

Despite a hectic social life across the salons and entertainments of Paris, Mucha still continued his prodigious output. Among advertising posters for clients such as Job cigarette papers, Nestlé's, Benedictine liqueur, Moet & Chandon champagne, and Cycles Perfecta to name but a few, he also made a series of decorative panels, each themed as four studies of voluptuous women, the Four Arts, the Four Times of Day, the Four Seasons, and the four Precious Stones. But this was not all: he designed a huge output of calendars, and book and magazine covers. He also sculpted, designed jewelry and ceramics and even fitted in regular seminars teaching students at the Académie Colarossi or in his own studio. With all this work he was making a great deal of money, but he spent it almost as quickly in extravagances and high living but also in lending to his less successful friends.

On December 20, 1899, Mucha published a limited edition of 510 copies of *Le Pater* (The Lord's Prayer), an occult examination of the themes of The Lord's Prayer and the work he considered to be his masterpiece.

The 1900 Universal Exhibition held in Paris gave Mucha's work real exposure. For the extravaganza he designed and decorated the walls of the Bosnia and Herzegovina pavilion with a series of huge historic Slavic paintings. He designed a poster for the Austrian pavilion and curated an exhibition for them. He also had a huge retrospective of his own work. The exhibition gave real exposure and momentum to the Art Nouveau movement that rapidly took western Europe by storm. For many people Mucha's work was the epitome of Art Nouveau, but it was a comparison that the artist himself refuted: he declared that his inspiration was of his own origin and owed nothing to anything except himself and Czech art. Like many artists both before and after him, Mucha felt his work was a noble calling and that his successful commercial work overshadowed his real talent that lay in his more private, spiritual and historic paintings.

Still anxious to prove his worth as a serious history painter, Mucha decided to travel to the United States to make a working tour and establish his reputation—while earning enough money to take home to Moravia where he could devote himself to painting the definitive story of the history of his people. Accordingly, in 1904 Mucha traveled to America and took up residence in New York City, where he tried his hand at portrait painting of such notables as the actress Leslie Carter, the cellist Zdenka Cerna, and his one-time compatriot the pianist and composer Rudolf Frimi.

His most prestigious commission was for the design of the German Theatre in New York, as well as sets and costumes for two Shakespearean productions there—but the theater closed within a year and he had to look elsewhere for work. For a while he taught drawing and composition at the Chicago Art Institute.

On returning to Europe, on June 10, 1906, Mucha married Maria (Maruška) Chytilová in Prague, then returned to America; their daughter Jaroslava was born in New York City. He still aimed to earn a comfortable living while gathering funds for nationalistic Czech projects. The latter was aided by millionaire businessman and philanthropist Charles R. Crane, who was also a financial sponsor of revolution and Slavic nationalism. He became Mucha's patron, in particular for his much-prized project, the Slav Epic.

In 1910 the Muchas returned to Prague where Mucha threw himself into commissions for various projects around the city including decorating the Theater of Fine Arts, and decorating the mayor's house at the Municipal House. Nine years later, at the conclusion of World War I, Czechoslovakia gained independence from the Austrian Empire, and as the country's most celebrated artist, Mucha was commissioned to design the new republic's banknotes and postage stamps as well as other government documents.

The Muchas had a son, Jiři, born on March 12, 1915, in Prague. He went on in later life to become a famous author, war correspondent, and his father's main publicist and supporter.

For much of his life Mucha dreamed of creating the *Slovanská epopej* (*Lépopée Slave* or The Slav Epic), a project he had envisaged since a boy. With the financial backing of Charles Crane he was able to realize his ambition. This huge enterprise entailed a series of twenty huge paintings celebrating the history of the Czech people in particular and the Slavs in general. It starts with "Slavs in their Original Homeland" and finishes with "Apotheosis of the Slavs." The canvases were vast, some up to eighteen feet tall. Mucha worked on the epic between 1912 and 1928 and the first eleven canvases went on public display in the Klementium in Prague in 1919. They were received with great enthusiasm and public acclaim, but the critics were harsher: they called the work dated and old-fashioned. Over the next twenty years the emerging canvases went on display in both America and Czechoslovakia, still to mixed public and critical reaction.

To research the project Mucha traveled extensively around the Balkans and Russia, and the result was thematically produced along cultural, religious, military, and allegorical lines. These in turn are broadly woven into three themes; a celebration of the virtues of the Slavs, lamentation over foreign oppressors and the wars they create, and finally a plea for Slavic unity.

In 1928 Mucha bequeathed the entire work to the city of Prague but the canvases were so large there was no obvious place to display them, much to Mucha's disappointment. The Epic briefly went on display in 1935 but then the canvases were rolled up and stored away and Mucha died believing that his greatest work was a failure. The paintings remained out of sight until 1963 when the first nine were exhibited and four years later the rest were put on display in the castle at Moravsky Krumlov.

In parts of 1930s Europe, especially Germany and Austria, the rise of fascism with its blatant anti-Slav racial policies meant that Mucha did not fit in well and led to reports of his work being reactionary. In spring 1939 German troops marched into Czechoslovakia and the Gestapo immediately rounded up all dissidents and intellectuals, including Mucha, although his artistic style had long fallen out of fashion. During his interrogation Mucha, now aged 79, fell ill with pneumonia. He was eventually released but the stress of the internment had taken its toll; he died in Prague on July 14, 1939. His death certificate noted that he died of a lung infection. He was buried in Vysehrad cemetery and it would be over twenty years and the advent of the Swinging Sixties before his work once more gained the appreciative audience it deserves.

Plate 1

GISMONDA

1894; 85 x 29.2 inch (216 × 74.2 cm); lithograph.
Private Collection

THE BULGARIAN TSAR SIMEON

1894; 189 x 159.4 inch (480 x 405 cm); egg tempera on canvas.
Prague, Czech Republic

Plate 2

THE CORONATION OF THE SERBIAN TSAR STEPAN DUSAN AS EAST ROMAN EMPEROR

1894; 189 x 159.4 inch (480 x 405 cm); egg tempera on canvas.
Prague, Czech Republic

Plate 3

AFTER THE BATTLE OF GRUNWALDU

1894; 240 x 159.4 inch (610 × 405 cm); egg tempera on canvas.
Prague, Czech Republic

Plate 4

MONT ATHOS

1894; 189 x 159.4 inch (480 x 405 cm); egg tempera on canvas.
Prague, Czech Republic

THE CELEBRATION OF SVANTOVIT

1894; 318 x 240 inch (810 × 610 cm); egg tempera on canvas. Prague, Czech Republic

Plate 6

THE MEETING AT KRIZKY

1894; 159.4 x 244 inch (405 × 620 cm); egg tempera on canvas.
Prague, Czech Republic

JAN MILIC OF KROMERIZ

1894; 159.4 x 244 inch (405 × 620 cm); egg tempera on canvas.
Prague, Czech Republic

Plate 8

THE LAST DAYS OF JAN AMOS KOMENSKY IN NAARDEN

1894; 244 x 159.4 inch (620 × 405 cm); egg tempera on canvas.

Prague, Czech Republic

PETR CHELCICKY AT VODNANY

1894; 244 x 159.4 inch (620 × 405 cm); egg tempera on canvas.
Prague, Czech Republic

Plate 10

THE PRINTING OF THE BIBLE OF KRALICE IN IVANCICE

1894; 318 x 240 inch (810 × 610 cm); egg tempera on canvas.
Prague, Czech Republic

LUCHON

1895; 41.6 x 29.6 inch (105.7 × 75.2 cm); lithograph
Private Collection

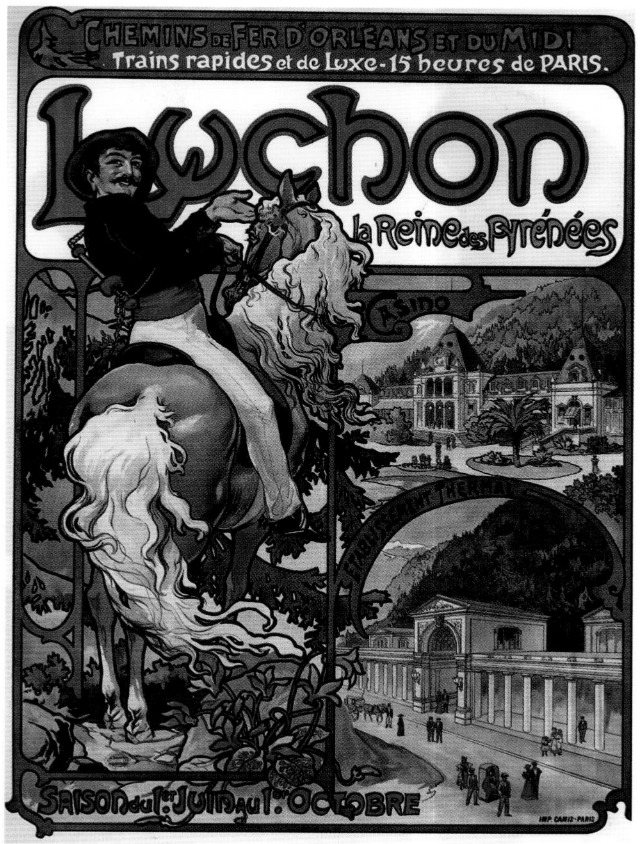

Plate 12

THE JUDGEMENT OF PARIS

1895; 19.6 x 12.8 inch (50 × 32.5 cm); mixed media.
Private Collection

PAUL GAUGIN IN MUCHAS STUDIO

1895; Photograph

Plate 14

AUTUMN

1896; 11 x 15.7 inch (28 x 14.5 cm); oil on panel
Private Collection

Plate 15

BISCUITS CHAMPAGNE LEFÈVRE UTILE

1896; 20.4 x 14 inch (52 × 35.5 cm); lithograph.
Private Collection

Plate 16

BISCUITS LEFÈVRE-UTILE

1896; 24.4 x 17.1 inch (62 × 43.5 cm); lithograph
Private Collection

THE LADY OF THE CAMELLIAS

1896; 80.1 x 28.7 inch (203.7 × 73 cm); lithograph.
Private Collection

Plate 18

LORENZACCIO

1896; 80.1 x 28.7 inch (203.7 × 73 cm); lithograph
Private Collection

SALAMMBÔ

1896; 15.3 x 8.4 inch (39 × 21.5 cm); lithograph.
Private Collection

Plate 20

SPRING

1896; oil on panel

Private Collection

SUMMER

1896; oil on panel.
Private Collection

Plate 22

WINTER

1896; oil on panel
Private Collection

JOB

1896; 26.2 x 18.2 inch (66.7 x 46.4 cm); lithograph
Private Collection

Plate 24

LANCE PARFUM RODO

1896; 26.2 x 19.5 inch (66.5 × 49.7 cm); lithograph.
Private Collection

Plate 25

THE INTRODUCTION OF THE SLAVONIC LITURGY

1896; 318 x 240 inch (810 × 610 cm); egg tempera on canvas.
Prague, Czech Republic

Plate 26

DEFENSE OF SZIGET AGAINST THE TURKS BY NICHOLAS ZRINSKY

1896; 318 x 240 inch (810 × 610 cm); egg tempera on canvas. Prague, Czech Republic

Plate 27

THE BOHEMIAN KING PREMYSL OTAKAR II

1896; 189 x 159.4 inch (480 x 405 cm); egg tempera on canvas.
Prague, Czech Republic

Plate 28

MASTER JAN HUS PREACHING AT THE BETHLEHEM CHAPEL V KAPLI BETLÉMSKÉ

1896; 318 x 240 inch (810 × 610 cm); egg tempera on canvas. Prague, Czech Republic

THE HUSSITE KING JIRI OF PODEBRAD

1896; 189 x 159.4 inch (480 x 405 cm); egg tempera on canvas.
Prague, Czech Republic

Plate 30

AFTER THE BATTLE OF VITKOV

1896; 189 x 159.4 inch (480 x 405 cm); egg tempera on canvas.
Prague, Czech Republic

Plate 31

THE OATH OF OMLADINA UNDER THE SLAVIC LINDEN TREE

1896; 189 x 159.4 inch (480 x 405 cm); egg tempera on canvas.
Prague, Czech Republic

Plate 32

FRUIT

1897; 26 x 17.5 inch (66.2 × 44.4 cm); lithograph.
Private Collection

MONACO MONTE CARLO

1897; 42.5 x 29.3 inch (108 × 74.5 cm); lithograph.
Private Collection

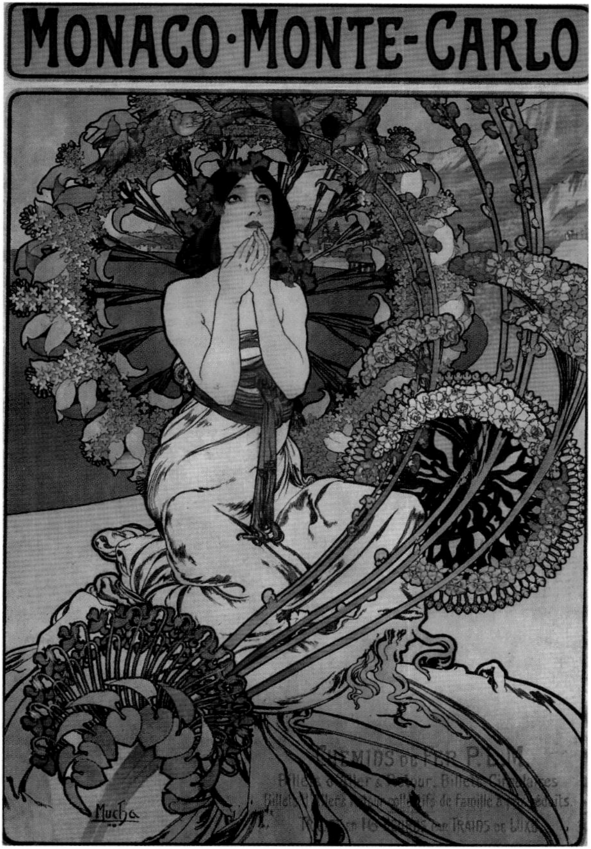

Plate 34

REVERIE

1897; 28.6 x 21.7 inch (72.7 x 55.2 cm); color-lithograph
Private Collection

F. CHAMPENOIS IMPRIMEUR-EDITEUR

1897; 28.6 x 21.7 inch (72.7 × 55.2 cm); lithograph
Private Collection

Plate 36

BIÈRES DE LA MEUSE

1897; 60.6 x 41.4 inch (154.5 × 104.5 cm); lithograph.
Private Collection

LA PLUME

1897; 9.8 x 7 inch (25 x 18 cm); lithograph.
Private Collection

Plate 38

LA TRAPPISTINE

1897; 81.1 x 30.3 inch (206 x 77 cm); watercolor
Suntory Ltd Collection, Osaka, Japan

NESTLÉ'S FOOD FOR INFANTS

1897; 28.3 x 13.5 inch (72 × 34.5 cm); lithograph
Private Collection

Plate 40

MEDEA

1898; 81.1 x 30 inch (206 × 76 cm); lithograph
Private Collection

THE ROSE

1898; 17 x 40.7 inch (43.3 x 103.5 cm); color-lithograph.
Private Collection

Plate 42

JOB CIGARETTE PAPERS

1898; 58.7 x 39.7 inch (149.2 x 101 cm); lithograph.
Private Collection

BÉNÉDICTINE

1898; 80.9 x 30.3 inch (205.7 × 77 cm); lithograph
Private Collection

Plate 44

DANCE

1898; 23.6 x 14.9 inch (60 x 38 cm) lithograph
Private Collection

PAINTING

1898; 23.6 x 14.9 inch (60 x 38 cm) lithograph
Private Collection

Plate 46

POETRY

1898; 23.6 x 14.9 inch (60 x 38 cm) lithograph
Private Collection

MUSIC

1898; 23.6 x 14.9 inch (60 x 38 cm) lithograph
Private Collection

Plate 48

ROSE

1898; 40.7 x 17 inch (103.5 × 43.3 cm); lithograph.
Private Collection

Plate 49

IRIS

1898; 40.7 x 17 inch (103.5 × 43.3 cm); lithograph.
Private Collection

Plate 50

CARNATION

1898; 40.7 x 17 inch (103.5 × 43.3 cm); lithograph.
Private Collection

LILY

1898; 40.7 x 17 inch (103.5 × 43.3 cm); lithograph.
Private Collection

Plate 52

MODEL POSING IN MUCHA'S STUDIO

1898; Photograph

HAMLET

1899; 81 x 30.1 inch (205.7 × 76.5 cm); lithograph.
Private Collection

Plate 54

MOËT & CHANDON CRÉMANT IMPÉRIAL

1899; 24 x 9 inch (60.8 × 23 cm); lithograph.
Private Collection

MOËT & CHANDON WHITE STAR

1899; 24 x 9 inch (60.8 × 23 cm); lithograph
Private Collection

Plate 56

MORNING AWAKENING

1899; 42.4 x 15.3 inch (107.7 × 39 cm); lithograph.
Private Collection

BRIGHTNESS OF DAY

1899; 42.4 x 15.3 inch (107.7 × 39 cm); lithograph.
Private Collection

Plate 58

EVENING CONTEMPLATION

1899; 42.4 x 15.3 inch (107.7 × 39 cm); lithograph.
Private Collection

NIGHT'S REST

1899; 42.4 x 15.3 inch (107.7 × 39 cm); lithograph.
Private Collection

Plate 60

IVY

1901; 21.6 x 23.4 inch (55 × 59.5 cm); lithograph.
Private Collection

LAUREL

1901; 21.6 x 23.4 inch (55 × 59.5 cm); lithograph.
Private Collection

Plate 62

HEIDSIECK & CO.

1901; 26.2 x 19.5 inch (66.5 × 49.7 cm); lithograph.
Private Collection

Plate 63

DESIGN FOR DOCUMENTS DECORATIFS PLATE 72

1902; 20.4 x 15.3 inch (52 x 39 cm) pencil and white on paper

Private Collection

Plate 64

HEATHER FROM COASTAL CLIFFS

1902; 29.1 x 13.7 inch (74 × 35 cm); lithograph.
Private Collection

CYCLES PERFECTA

1902; 60.8 x 41 inch (154.6 × 104.3 cm); lithograph
Private Collection

Plate 66

THE RED CAPE

1902; 19.2 x 25.5 inch (48.8 × 64.8 cm); oil on canvas
Private Collection

ST LOUIS WORLDS FAIR

1904; lithograph.
Private Collection

Plate 68

MORAVIAN TEACHERS' CHOIR

1911; 42.7 x 31.3 (108.5 × 79.5 cm); lithograph.
Private Collection

THE SLAVS IN THEIR ORIGINAL HOMELAND

1912; 318 x 240 inch (810 × 610 cm); egg tempera on canvas.
Prague, Czech Republic.

Plate 70

LOTTERY OF NATIONAL UNITY

1912; 50.3 x 37.4 in (128 × 95 cm); lithograph.

THE ABOLITION OF SERFDOM IN RUSSIA

1914; 318 x 240 inch (810 × 610 cm); egg tempera on canvas.
Prague, Czech Republic

Plate 72

GIRL WITH LOOSE HAIR AND TULIPS

1920; 30.2 x 26.3 inch (76.8 x 66.9 cm); oil on canvas

THE APOTHEOSIS OF THE SLAVS

1926; 159.4 x 189 inch (405 x 480 cm); egg tempera on canvas.
Prague, Czech Republic

Plate 74

WOMAN WITH A BURNING CANDLE

1933; 30.7 x 31.1 inch (78 x 79 cm); oil on canvas.
Private Collection

SEATED WOMAN WITH COFFEE CUP

age unknown; watercolor.
Private Collection